Every night is Saturday Night!

CONTENTS

Edited by CECIL BOLTON

First Published 1988
© International Music Publications Limited,
Southend Road, Woodford Green,
Essex IG8 8HN, England.

*Front Cover Photograph reproduced by kind
permission of Hollywoods, Romford.*

215-2-480

Medley 1

ROCK AROUND THE CLOCK

Words and Music by
MAX C. FREEDMAN and JIMMY DAKNIGHT

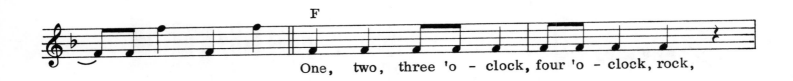

One,   two,   three 'o - clock, four 'o - clock, rock,

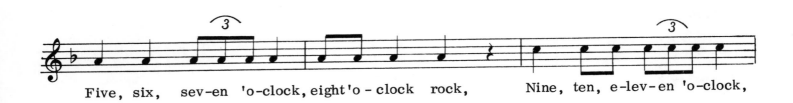

Five,   six,   sev-en 'o-clock, eight 'o - clock rock,   Nine, ten, e-lev-en 'o-clock,

Twelve 'o - clock   rock, We're gon - na   rock   a - round   the

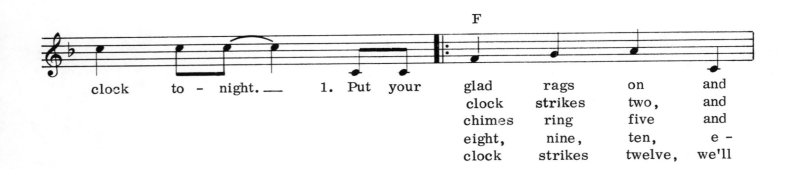

clock   to - night. ___   1. Put   your   glad   rags   on   and
clock   strikes   two,   and
chimes   ring   five   and
eight,   nine,   ten,   e -
clock   strikes   twelve,   we'll

join me, hon, ____ We'll have some fun when the
three and four, ____ If the band slows down we'll
six and seven, ____ We'll be rock - in' up in
-lev - en, too, ____ I'll be go - in' strong and
cool off, then, ____ Start a - rock - in' 'round the

clock strikes one, ____
yell for more, ____
sev - enth heav'n, ____ } We're gon - na rock a - round the
so will you, ____
clock a - gain, ____

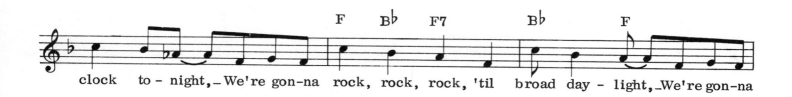

clock to - night,—We're gon-na rock, rock, rock, 'til broad day - light,—We're gon-na

rock, gon - na rock a - round ____ the clock ____ to - night.

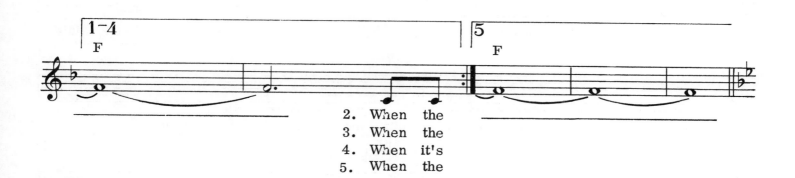

2. When the
3. When the
4. When it's
5. When the

HOUND DOG

Words and Music by
JERRY LEIBER and MIKE STOLLER

Medley 2

LOVE LETTERS IN THE SAND

Words by NICK KENNY and CHARLES KENNY
Music by J. FRED COOTS

WHO'S SORRY NOW

Words by HARRY RUBY and BERT KALMAR
Music by TED SNYDER

DIANA

Words and Music by
PAUL ANKA

CRY

Words and Music by
CHURCHILL KOHLMAN

Medley 3

ONLY YOU

Words and Music by
BUCK RAM and ANDE RAND

MY PRAYER

English Lyrics by JIMMY KENNEDY
Music by GEORGES BOULANGER

prayer ___ is to lin-ger with you, ___ At the end of the day, ___ in a dream that's di-vine. ___ My prayer ___ is a rap-ture in blue, ___ With the world far a- -way, ___ and your lips close to mine. ___ To- -night ___ while our hearts are a-glow, ___ Oh, tell me the words ___ that I'm long-ing to know. ___ My prayer ___ and the ans-wer you give, ___ May they still be the same, ___ for as long as we live, ___ That you'll al-ways be there, ___ at the end of my prayer. ___ I saw the

HARBOUR LIGHTS

Words by JIMMY KENNEDY
Music by WILHELM GROSZ

THE GREAT PRETENDER

Words and Music by
BUCK RAM

Medley 4

JAILHOUSE ROCK

Words and Music by
JERRY LEIBER and MIKE STOLLER

1. The war-den threw a par-ty in the coun-ty jail,___ The
2. Spi-der Mur-phy play'd the ten-or sax-o-phone,___ The
3. Num-ber For-ty-sev-en said to Num-ber Three,___ The

pri-son band was there and they be-gan to wail.__ The
Lit-tle Joe was blow-in' on the slide trom-bone.__ The
"You're the cut-est jail-bird I ev-er did see.__ I

band was jump-in' and the joint be-gan to swing,___ You
drum-mer boy from Il-li-nois went crash, boom, bang!__ The
sure would be de-light-ed with your com-pa-ny. ___ Come

should-'ve heard those knock-out jail-birds sing.__ Let's
whole ____ rhy-thm sec-tion was the pur-ple gang.__ Let's
on and do the Jail-house Rock with me."__

rock!   Let's rock!

Ev-'ry-bo-dy in the whole cell block __ was a

danc-in' to the Jail-House Rock!__

THE LOCO-MOTION

Words and Music by
GERRY GOFFIN and CAROLE KING

Ev-'ry-bod-y's do - in' a brand new dance now. C'm on, ba-by, do

The Lo-co-Mo - tion. I know you'll get to like it if you give it a chance now.

C'm on, ba-by, do The Lo-co-Mo - tion. My lit-tle ba-by sis - ter can

do it with ease, It's eas-i-er than learn - in' your A B Cs, So

come on, come on, do The Lo-co-Mo-tion with me. You got-ta

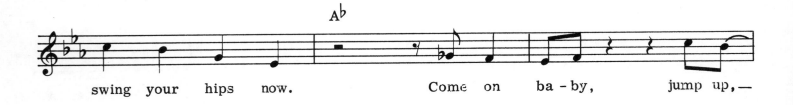

swing your hips now. Come on ba - by, jump up,

jump back, Oh well, I think you got the knack.

ROCKIN' ALL OVER THE WORLD

Words and Music by
JOHN FOGERTY

Medley 5

LIVING DOLL

Words and Music by
LIONEL BART

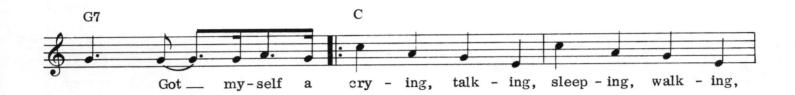

Got __ my-self a cry - ing, talk - ing, sleep - ing, walk - ing,

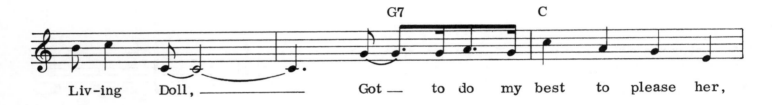

Liv-ing Doll, _____ Got __ to do my best to please her,

just 'cos she's a Liv - ing Doll. _____ Such __ a rov - ing

eye, and that is why she sat - is - fies my soul, ___

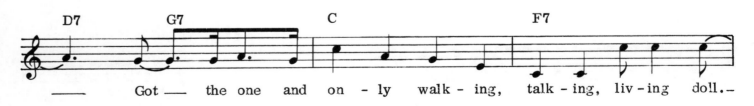

Got __ the one and on - ly walk - ing, talk - ing, liv - ing doll.__

Got __ my-self a _____ The

THE YOUNG ONES

Words and Music by
ROY BENNETT and SID TEPPER

BACHELOR BOY

Words and Music by
BRUCE WELCH and CLIFF RICHARD

When I was young ___ my fath - er said "Son I have

some - thing to say." ___ And what he told me I'll

nev - er for - get un - til my dy - in' day.

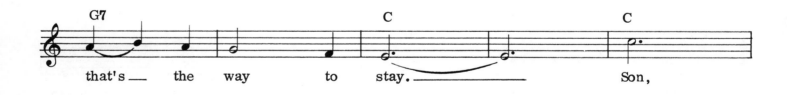

He ___ said "Son, you are a bach - el - or boy and

that's ___ the way to stay. ___ Son,

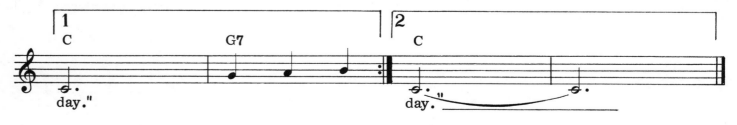

you be a bach - el - or boy un - til your dy - in'

1
day."

2
day." ___

Medley 6

HANDFUL OF SONGS

Words and Music by
MICHAEL PRATT, TOMMY STEELE
and LIONEL BART

I've got a hand-ful of songs to sing — you, Can't stop my voice when it
More-ov-er wher-ev-er we may roam — to, Or an-y shore where we

longs to sing — you, New songs, and blue songs and songs to bring — you
may be blown — to, We'll know that we're gon-na feel at home — to

hap-pi-ness, — no more, no less.— La Bel-la — Mus-i-ca. —

Jazz — and cha cha cha,— Ca-lyp-sos and street ven-dors cries.

Strains of old re-frains,— sleep-y time ba-by lul-la-bies.—

I've got a hand-ful of songs to sing — you, I've got a heart-ful of love to bring — you,

True love for you love, and love's a thing — you keep, — So here's a

hand-ful of songs — go-ing cheap. To spend one

THAT'S MY DESIRE

Words and Music by
CARROLL LOVEDAY and HELMA KRESA

I HEAR YOU KNOCKIN'

Words and Music by
DAVE BARTHOLOMEW and PEARL KING

Medley 7

ARE YOU LONESOME TONIGHT

Words and Music by
ROY TURK and LOU HANDMAN

TEARS

Words by FRANK CAPANO
Music by BILLY URH

Tears for sou-ven-irs are all you left me,
Mem-'ries of a love you nev-er meant.
I just can't be-lieve you could for-get me,
Af-ter all the hap-py hours we spent to-geth-er.
Tears have been my on-ly con-so-la-tion, But tears can't mend a bro-ken heart I must con-fess. Let's for-give and for-get, Turn our tears of re-gret, Once more to tears of hap-pi-ness.
I

TRUE LOVE

Words and Music by
COLE PORTER

Medley 8

CHANSON D'AMOUR (SONG OF LOVE)

Words and Music by
WAYNE SHANKLIN

HAPPINESS

Words and Music by
BILL ANDERSON

ISN'T SHE LOVELY

Words and Music by
STEVIE WONDER

Medley 9

LET'S TWIST AGAIN

Words and Music by
KAL MANN and DAVE APPELL

MOVE IT

Words and Music by
IAN SAMWELL

Blue Suede Shoes

Words and Music by
CARL LEE PERKINS

Medley 10

MA (HE'S MAKING EYES AT ME)

Words by SIDNEY CLARE
Music by CON CONRAD

"Ma" _____ he's mak-ing

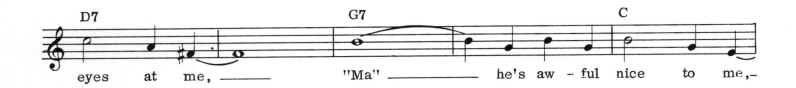

eyes at me, _____ "Ma" _____ he's aw-ful nice to me,—

_____ "Ma" he's al-most break-ing my heart, _____

I'm be-side him, Mer-cy let his con-science guide him, "Ma" _____

— he wants to mar-ry me, _____ Be my hon-ey

bee, _____ Ev-'ry min-ute he gets bold-er, Now he's lean-ing

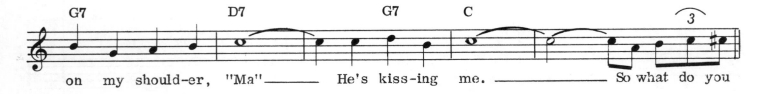

on my shoul-der, "Ma" _____ He's kiss-ing me. _____ So what do you

WHAT DO YOU WANT TO MAKE THOSE EYES AT ME FOR?

Words and Music by
JOSEPH McCARTHY, HOWARD JOHNSON
and JIMMY V. MONACO

want to make those eyes at me for, When they don't mean what they

say? _____ They make me glad, _____ They make me sad, _____ They

make me want a lot of things I've nev - er had. _____ So what do you

want to fool a - round with me for? You lead me on and then you run a-

- way. _____ But nev - er mind, I'll get you a-lone some night and then you'll

sure - ly find, you're flirt-ing with dy - na-mite, So what do you want to make those eyes at

me for, When they don't mean what they say? _____

I REMEMBER YOU

Words by JOHNNY MERCER
Music by VICTOR SCHERTZINGER

HE'S GOT THE WHOLE WORLD IN HIS HANDS

Arranged by
CECIL BOLTON and CHRIS ELLIS

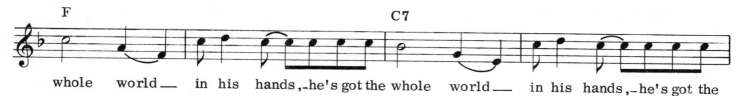

whole world — in his hands, —he's got the whole world — in his hands, —he's got the

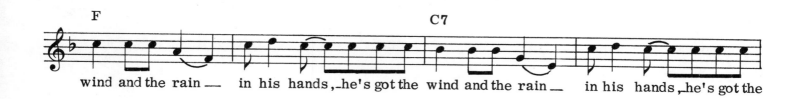

whole world — in his hands, —he's got the whole world in his hands. — He's got the

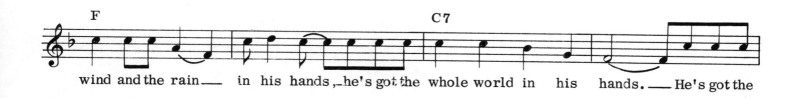

wind and the rain — in his hands, —he's got the wind and the rain — in his hands, he's got the

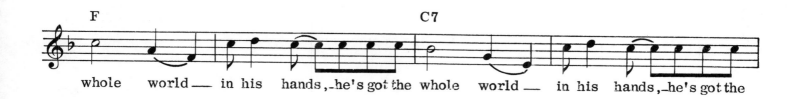

wind and the rain — in his hands, —he's got the whole world in his hands. — He's got the

whole world — in his hands, —he's got the whole world — in his hands, —he's got the

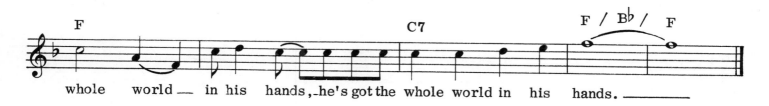

whole world — in his hands, —he's got the whole world in his hands. —

Medley 11

BANANA BOAT SONG

Words and Music by
ERIK DARLING, BOB CAREY
and ALAN ARKIN

SLOOP JOHN B.

Arranged by
CECIL BOLTON and CHRIS ELLIS

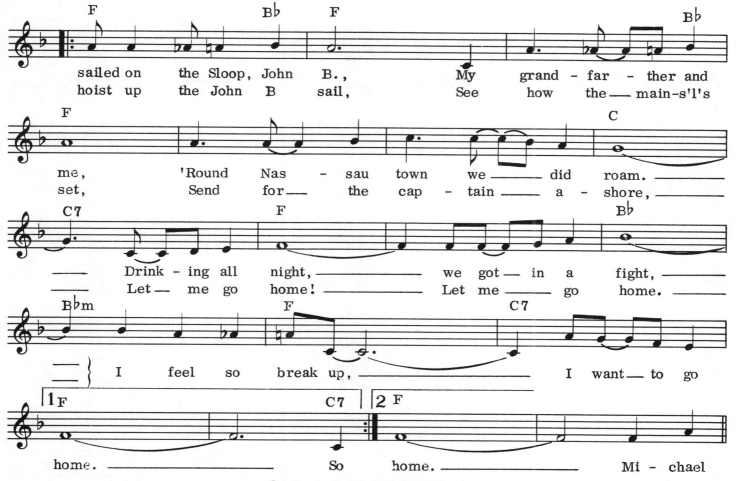

sailed on the Sloop, John B., My grand - far - ther and
hoist up the John B sail, See how the — main-s'l's

me, 'Round Nas - sau town we — did roam. —
set, Send for — the cap - tain — a - shore,

Drink - ing all night, — we got — in a fight, —
Let — me go home! — Let me — go home. —

I feel so break up, — I want — to go

home. — So home. — Mi - chael

MICHAEL ROW THE BOAT

Arranged by
CECIL BOLTON and CHRIS ELLIS

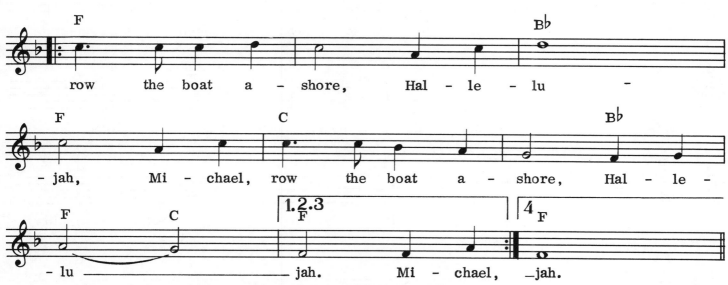

row the boat a - shore, Hal - le - lu -

- jah, Mi - chael, row the boat a - shore, Hal - le -

- lu — jah. Mi - chael, —jah.

2. Sister help to trim the sail,
Hallelujah,
Sister help to trim the sail,
Hallelujah.

3. Jordan's river is deep and wide,
Hallelujah,
Meet my mother on the other side,
Hallelujah.

4. Michael row the boat ashore,
Hallelujah,
Michael row the boat ashore,
Hallelujah.

YELLOW BIRD

Words by ALAN BERGMAN and MARILYN KEITH
Music by NORMAN LUBOFF

ISLAND IN THE SUN

Words and Music by
HARRY BELAFONTE and LORD BURGESS

Medley 12

SINGING THE BLUES

Words and Music
MELVIN ENDSL

Well I

nev-er felt more like sing-ing the blues,— 'cause I nev-er thought— tha
nev-er felt more like cry-ing all night,— 'cause ev-'ry-thing's wrong— an

I'd ev-er lose— your love, dear, Why'd you do me this way? —
noth-ing ain't right— with-out you,

Well, I You got me sing-ing the blues. — The

moon and stars no long-er shine, the dream is gone I thought was mine, Ther

noth-ing left for me to do but cry —

o-ver you.— Well, I nev-er felt more like run-ning a-way,— bu

why should I go — 'cause I could-n't stay — with-out you,

You got me sing-ing the blues.

HAPPY BIRTHDAY SWEET SIXTEEN

Words and Music by
NEIL SEDAKA and HOWARD GREENFIELD

thir - teen ____ you were my fun - ny val - en - tine. ____ But

since you've grown up your fu - ture is sown up, From now on you're

gon-na be mine; So, If I should smile ____ with sweet sur-prise,

____ It's just that you've grown up be - fore my ve - ry

eyes. You've turned in - to the pret - ti - est girl I've ev - er

seen. ____ Hap - py Birth - day Sweet Six - teen. ____

BIMBO

Words and Music by
ROD MORRIS

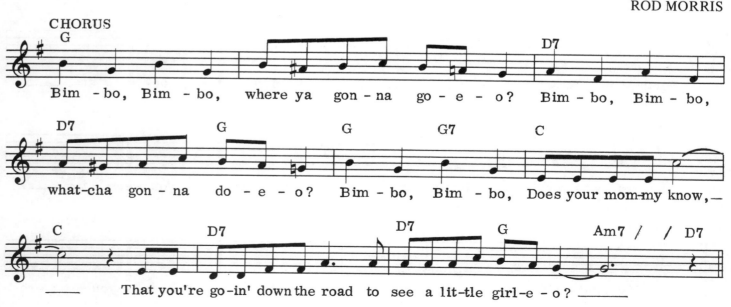

CHORUS

Bim - bo, Bim - bo, where ya gon - na go - e - o? Bim - bo, Bim - bo,

what-cha gon - na do - e - o? Bim - bo, Bim - bo, Does your mom-my know, ____

____ That you're go-in' down the road to see a lit-tle girl - e - o? ____

45

Medley 13

RED SAILS IN THE SUNSET

Words by JIMMY KENNEDY
Music by WILHELM GROSZ

Red sails in the sun - set, 'Way out on the sea,

Oh, car - ry my lov'd one home safe - ly to me.

He sail'd at the dawn - ing, all day I've been blue,

Red sails in the sun - set, I'm trust - ing in you.

Swift wings you must bor - row, Make straight for the shore.

We mar - ry to - mor - row, And he goes sail - ing no more.

Red sails in the sun - set, 'Way out on the sea,

Oh, car - ry my lov'd one home safe - ly to me. I found my

BLUEBERRY HILL

Words and Music by
AL LEWIS, LARRY LAWRENCE STOCK and VINCENT ROSE

thrill _____ on Blue-ber-ry Hill, _____ On Blue-ber-ry
Hill, _____ when I found you. _____ The moon stood
still, _____ on Blue-ber-ry Hill, _____ And lin-gered un-
til _____ my dreams came true. _____ The wind in the
wil - low played _____ love's sweet mel-o - dy, _____ But all of those
vows we made _____ were nev-er to be. _____ Tho' we're a-
part, _____ you're part of me still, _____ For you were my
thrill, _____ on Blue-ber-ry Hill. _____

I'M IN LOVE AGAIN

Words and Music by
ANTOINE DOMINO and DAVE BARTHOLOMEW

AIN'T THAT A SHAME

Words and Music by
ANTOINE DOMINO and DAVE BARTHOLOMEW

Medley 14

SEE YOU LATER ALLIGATOR

Words and Music by
ROBERT GUIDRY

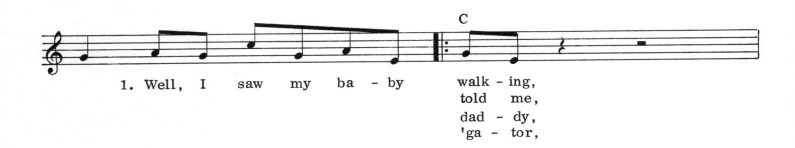

1. Well, I saw my ba - by walk - ing,
told me,
dad - dy,
'ga - tor,

With an - oth - er man to - day, ——
Near - ly made me lose my head, ——
You know my love is just for you, ——
I know you meant it just for play, ——

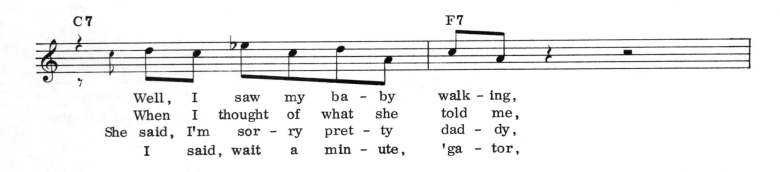

Well, I saw my ba - by walk - ing,
When I thought of what she told me,
She said, I'm sor - ry pret - ty dad - dy,
I said, wait a min - ute, 'ga - tor,

With an - oth - er man to - day, ——
Near - ly made me lose my head, ——
You know my love is just for you, ——
I know you meant it just for play, ——

BYE BYE, LOVE

Words and Music by
BOUDLEAUX BRYAND and FELICE BRYANT

ROCK AROUND THE CLOCK

Words and Music by
MAX C. FREEDMAN and JIMMY DAKNIGHT

One, two, three 'o - clock, four 'o - clock rock, Five, six, sev-en 'o-clock

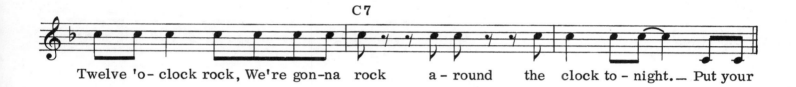

eight 'o - clock rock, Nine, ten, e - lev-en 'o - clock

Twelve 'o- clock rock, We're gon-na rock a - round the clock to - night.__ Put your

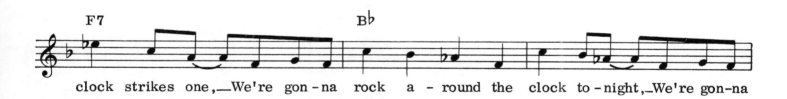

glad rags on and join me hon,__ We'll have some fun when the

clock strikes one,__ We're gon -na rock a - round the clock to - night,__ We're gon -na

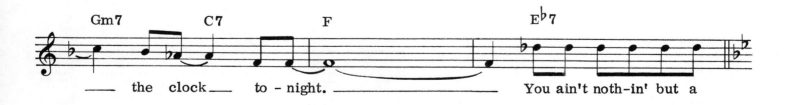

rock, rock, rock, 'til broad day - light,__ We're gon-na rock, gon-na rock a - round__

the clock__ to - night. _____ You ain't noth-in' but a

HOUND DOG

Words and Music by
JERRY LEIBER and MIKE STOLLER

BLUE SUEDE SHOES

Words and Music by
CARL LEE PERKINS

LET'S TWIST AGAIN

Words and Music by
KAL MANN and DAVE APPELL